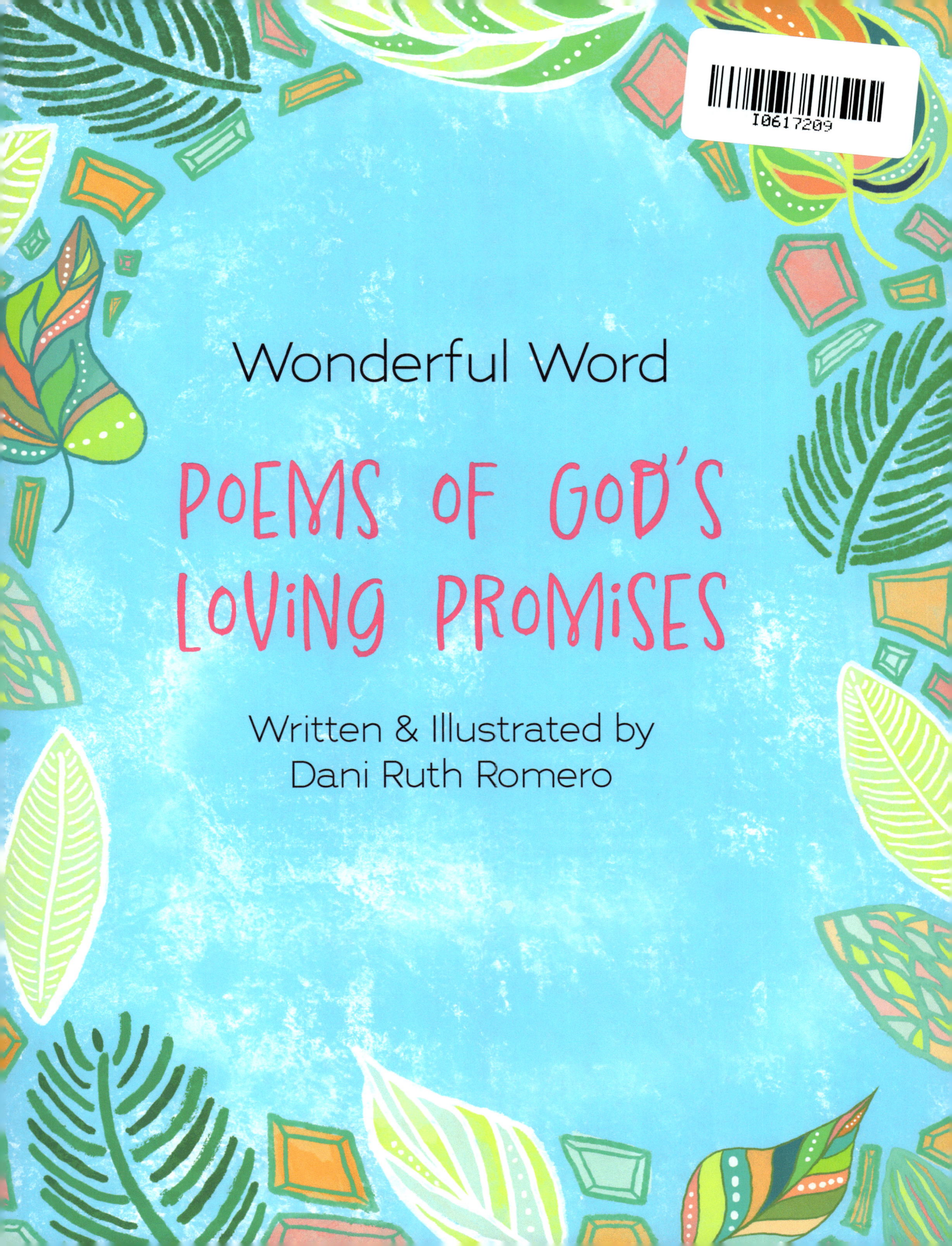

Wonderful Word

POEMS OF GOD'S LOVING PROMISES

Written & Illustrated by
Dani Ruth Romero

Briley & Baxter Publications | Plymouth, Massachusetts

All Scripture in this publication is inspired by the Holy Bible, New
International Version ®, NIV ®

Hardcover ISBN: 978-1-954819-73-3
Paperback ISBN: 978-1-954819-75-7

Photography of Dani & David captured by Rae Curtis

For information contact dani@rrillustration.com | www.rrillustration.com
Instagram: @ruthieromero_illustration

DEDICATED TO MY AWESOME HUSBAND DAVID

How God's ways are always higher,
Exceedingly far above mine...
So much that He gave me you:
A man after God's own heart!

You are a pure reflection of His light,
A vessel that radiates joy, vitality, & boldness.
Your constant encouragement gives me the liberty to be,
The woman God created me to be,
So I could pursue the dreams He's placed within my heart.

You truly are a treasure!
A fulfilled promise by our Loving King,
Leaving me only to discover,
That God alone knows exactly what I need!

CONTENTS

A GLORIOUS MISSION

In my quiet time with the Lord, both in moments of prayer & worship,
I would find my mind overflowing with creative imagery...
Knowing that this was not my own imagination,
But something that came like a gift from The King...

As I took the time to draw the things I'd see,
Various scripture would begin to flow within me simultaneously.
Little did I know that The Lord was creating & weaving together something so beautiful,
A tangible expression of my heart's worship,
Illustrated books coming to life, in a way to share with all mankind.

It is my greatest desire that these illustrated poems of praise & worship
would be a source of divine encouragement,
Stirring the hearts of not only children, but of all ages,
To seek more after the true heart of this incredible King
Being free to receive all He has in store with child-like faith:
All hope & joy unleashed for those who believe

Oh, wait!
One more thing....
Last but not least,
I pray that this book will open eyes to see the Bible in a new & exciting way,
Standing with a newfound awe & wonder of the living Word of God.

Thanks for Reading!
Dani Ruth Romero

LAYING THE GROUNDWORK FOR WONDERFUL WORD: POEMS OF GOD'S LOVING PROMISES

It was the start of 2020—so much initial hope & excitement for a new decade ahead. Anticipation was stirring within me for God to come through with some of my heart's greatest desires as I looked at the new year before me. But what came prowling to the world's surprise? COVID-19. A plague of fear & terror swept the planet. Feelings of isolation & discouragement covered the nation, leaving many wondering how God was going to use this in His plan for good.

During this season of so many unknowns in my life, something new was around the corner. Sitting alone in my studio apartment, new creativity swept in my spirit. God gave me a new assignment: to set my focus on His love & promises.

Full of excitement to ride the waves in His sea of creativity, I knew in my heart that this book would end with the result of a fulfilled personal promise—one I'd been believing for what felt like a life-time…The promise of a husband!

As I believed what God was revealing to me, my heart of doubt quickly responded. There was not a man in sight for me to have faith for this promise! Yet I felt God's gentle smile upon me, knowing He was working something special behind the scenes…

A couple months later, God brought David into my life: a friendly and familiar face I'd see around my church—a man of God's joy & light. Never thinking he'd be the one that would become my husband! Friendship came first, then the growing love for one another. All the more as we continued to put God first in our relationship.

It wasn't long after that summer—just five months later, that he'd take me up to the Smoky Mountains, asking me to be his wife! Here we are, just two years later…

This book is now completed & I am married to David
A dream fulfilled—how it is a tree of life
May this book give you hope & encouragement
In how our amazing God provides!
Even a malicious pandemic can't box in all of His unfailing love & promises!
—Dani Ruth Romero

HOPE IS LIKE AN EMERALD TREE

Oh my Lord,
How precious is Your gift of hope!
When there is none around me,
Life can look dark & gloomy.

By reading Your word,
You bring comfort to my heart.
Encouraging me to have faith for the things unseen,
All with a confident expectation in who You are.
For You are a God that does wonders beyond imagination,
Known for the multitudes of miracles too numerous to count.

Your hope restores the way I see life,
How everything is brighter & lighter.
A desire fulfilled by You is like a vibrant tree of life,
One exploding with gems of emerald color,
Because You alone are the true treasure of life.

I love who You are, My beautiful King,
How You only show unfailing love & goodness towards me.
Those who put their hope in You will never be put to shame!

Inspired Scripture: Proverbs 13:12, Romans 8:24-25, Job 5:9, Psalm 25:3

No Limits With You

Your love, oh Lord, it reaches to the heavens!
How there is no height nor depth,
Length or width.

How this wondrous love knows no limits!
Nothing can separate me from it.
If I were to flee to the highest place this world has seen,
Still Your love would be there,
Gently waiting to enclose me in Your unfailing goodness.

I praise You for Your love.
I praise You for Your promise:
That You will faithfully pursue me all the days of my life,
With Your everlasting goodness.

Inspired Scriptures: Psalm 36:5-7, Ephesians 3:18-19, Romans 8:35-39, Psalm 23:6

TURTLE ADVENTURE

Praise, Praise!
For it is a new day!
Adventure is waiting,
All in this amazing day spent with The King.

A fresh outpouring of Your love,
Is what I desire to receive.
How it cleanses my mind,
Anticipating all the good You're about to bring.

More adventures we desire,
When we seek after You!
Let us go, oh Lord!
Let us go after the things of You!

Inspired Scripture: Psalm 118:24, Romans 15:13

CROCODILES GET GIFTS TOO

I thank You Lord that You are a God that loves to give;
There is no one that can out-give You!
This I know to be true:
That every good & perfect gift comes from You!

As much as I cherish these gifts,
You speak that they are to be given to others.
For to whom it is given,
Much is required.

Your heart rejoices when we happily give to others,
With the measure that we use, it will be given back to us as well.
May we give good gifts to others,
With a heart that purely reflects our Heavenly Father.

Inspired Scripture: 2 Corinthians 9:7-8, James 1:17, Luke 12:48

OCEAN DEPTHS of YOUR LOVE

There is nothing I can do that can separate me from this great sea of love,
For You are the one that keeps no record of wrong.
Your kindness & compassion are not gifts from afar,
Grace upon grace is lavished upon me;
This is the God that You are!

Your blessings make me rich with the fullness of life.
Companionship & community are gifts from above.
I thank You, Lord, for all the amazing people You have put in my life!

I praise You, my King,
For all the celebrations ahead with my friends,
Giving thanks to You for all the amazing things You have done!

Inspired Scripture: Proverbs 10:22, Hebrews 10:22-24

A SLOTH'S PROMISE

Oh my Lord, I am weary & tired,
My feet drag,
& my heart is a little sad...

You say believe as if you've received,
& it shall be done,
But I can't see anything!

It is known from long ago,
That when You come,
You certainly won't delay,
All of the glorious things You have in store.

Your love rains down refreshing rest,
Lifting me from this mopey pit.

By this goodness You give,
I am renewed & revived.
How You are faithful to fill all my years with good things,
More than I could ever describe!

I will tell of the wondrous things You have accomplished for me,
Knowing that it was You alone who fulfilled the desires of my heart.
For You, oh Lord, always dream more for me.
How Your path is the way to true life!

Inspired scripture: Mark 11:24, Hebrews 10:36-38, Psalm 103:1-5,
Psalm 16:11, John 14:5-6

THE PACE OF GRACE

Today we run our race,
Keeping in step with The King's pace of grace.
Setting our gaze forward,
With motivated hearts to live our lives for You.

May we not run for a temporary medal,
But the eternal prize,
Of living with You forevermore!

Keep us anchored in Your hope,
& grounded in Your love,
Knowing that what You have in store for our lives,
Is so high above!

May we not get discouraged,
Nor lose our focus.
Cause in the end,
You always work it all out for our good,
Always for Your greater purpose!

Inspired Scriptures: Hebrews 12:1-3, 1 Corinthians 9:24-27, Romans 8:28,
Hebrews 10:36-38, Hebrews 6:19-20

LAND OF LOVE

My heart is ever devoted to You, oh my Loving King!
How You came through for me,
In a great & mighty way!

You saw the life I was living,
One that really wasn't a life at all.
How it was full of striving & trying to make things work all on my own!

You saw the aches & pains of my heart,
& all the tears rolling down my eyes.
Yet You call me Your heart's delight,
Desiring something greater for my life.

You took me under Your wing, swooping me away,
Asking me to have just a little bit of faith,
So that I could move forward in Your better ways.

How You took me into a spacious place,
To a land flowing with milk & honey.
A place of healing & restoration,
Where You knew I'd be able to do all sorts of wondrous things,
Running toward my wildest of dreams!

This is my heart's latest & greatest desire:
That I would become a pure reflection & extension of Your love,
Telling the ends of the earth,
Of the wonderful God that You are!

Inspired Scripture: Psalm 57:7-11, Psalm 108:1-5, Deuteronomy 7:10,
Colossians 3:17, 1 Corinthians 10:31

THE GREATEST GIFT OF ALL

A beautiful gift You have given, oh Lord,
A love that knows no limits.
Bringing a fullness of life,
Something I can't even begin to describe!

New mercies for today,
& hope for tomorrow.
How Your sweet love is a promise that brings new life!

You love to lavish us with good gifts,
Wrapped in joy & hope.
But the greatest gift of all,
Is Your unfailing love.

This love surpasses all borders,
How there is no height, depth, or way to measure,
There's no box that can contain it!

But what is love if I keep it to myself?
Freely I have received,
So freely I can give it away.
After all, this love knows no limits!

Inspired Scripture: Ephesians 3:18-19, 1 Corinthians 13:13, Matthew 10:5-8,
Lamentations 3:22-24, James 1:17

LOVE FOR A LiTTLE LEMUR

A God of Healing,
Is who You are.
With a mighty & outstretched hand,
You placed me on the path to new life.

Beauty for ashes You have given,
Leading me to a place of overflow.
All wrapped in Your healing,
Just so I could discover the true God that You are.

Your friendship outweighs any treasure,
Because of Your great goodness,
I am now free to discover all the things You have always desired,
Which was to give me the fullness of life

Here's to the path of living with You forever,
My God of great healing & delight!

Inspired Scripture: John 10:10, Deuteronomy 26:8-9, Psalm 103, Isaiah 61

LOVE BEARS ALL THiNGS

Your love, Our King,
It bears all things.
What does this mean?

It is You who always sees the best in me,
Pointing out all of the treasure You have placed within my heart.
You are so gentle & patient when I am grumpy,
& faithful to forgive when I make mistakes.

Because of this unfailing love You have for me,
You tell me to I am to love others just like You love me.
How this is the love You desired from the start!
For Your love, oh Lord,
How it bears all things.

Inspired Scripture: 1 Corinthians 13 Ephesians 4:1-3, Hebrews 13, Proverbs
10:12, Romans 8:37-39, John 13:34

LACK NO GOOD THING

Thank You, my Lord!
I will never lack with You,
How You own everything,
Both in heaven & on earth.

Sometimes the lions lack food & get hungry,
But You are faithful to promise,
That those who look to You to care for their lives,
Will have all they need & more!

Inspired Scriptures: Deuteronomy 10:14, Psalm 24::1-2, John 14:1-9,
Matthew 6:25-34, Psalm 34:8-10, 1 John 5:14-15

ONLY THE BEST

I am Your child,
I am Your friend.
Greater love has no one than this,
That He would lay down His life for His friend.

How can it be?
That You would give Jesus for me?
Just so I can be called Your friend?

What do You desire of me?
To love just like You,
Unselfishly seeking the best for others,
& giving my absolute best.
All as if it were for You!

You are so good to us, our Lord;
May we learn to serve one another only with our best,
As it were for You,
The Great & Mighty King!

Inspired Scriptures: John 15:12, Psalm 103:11, Ephesians 5:1-2, 1 John 4:7-21

AN OCEAN PRAiSE

Today we play,
Today we sing,
Praising You for Your goodness,
Promising a love that will never leave!

The rocks cry out,
The oceans roar & quake,
All in response,
To the glory of Your Great Name.

Because of Your great love,
We are not consumed.
Even when seasons of life get stormy,
May we never forget that You're the one that always comes through.

Seas will part,
Rocks gush forth water,
& the bread of heaven rains down from the skies!
These tangible signs were designed for us to see,
That You are the Miraculous God of Wonder.

Our loving Lord, there is nothing You can't do!
What is impossible with man,
Is always possible with You!

Inspired Scripture: Isaiah 54:10, Psalm 89:1-4, Exodus 14:15-31,
Exodus 17:1-7, Exodus 16, Luke 18:27

A PRAiSE FOR THE DAY AHEAD

Good morning, my sweet King!
How Your life-changing love gives me excitement to rise from my bed.
I can't wait to see all the wonderful things You have planned for this day ahead!

From breakfast to lunch,
& the time I play with my friends,
You're always faithful to be one step ahead!

Just like the birds of the air,
You already know my needs.
You know every word on my tongue,
& all the thoughts that pass through my brain!

I sit to consider You, my glorious King...
All of Your wondrous works,
& Your vibrant creation.
How all the earth will sing of the good father that You are to Your children!

Inspired Scripture: Psalm 139:1-6, Matthew 6:25-34, Psalm 145:16

PEACEFUL OCEANS

Oh Lord, I will not be afraid nor anxious,
Because it is here I find peace in Your presence.

Your promise of unfailing mercy & goodness,
Is faithful to pursue me each moment.
I am immersed in Your sea of love,
Sailing upon Your waves of kindness.

This one thing I'd like to ask of my faithful King,
That You will show me how to dwell more with You each day.

How I will rest secure in all that You are,
For apart from The King,
I truly have no good thing!

Inspired Scripture: Luke 12:32, Matthew 16:19, Psalm 16,
Psalm 27:4, Psalm 23:6

No Fear in Love

Oh Lord, there're days I am afraid,
& times I feel so scared,
How it makes me not want to leave my bed!

When I crouch down & start praying to You,
You quiet my mind...
Gently reminding me the promises of You.

No fear exists in the depths of Your love,
Perfect peace You have given me,
As I keep my mind centered on You.

This peace is forever mine to keep,
It's something that I can't describe.
It calms me in any circumstance,
Giving me the courage You spoke it would provide.

I thank You for Your unfailing promises to me, my loving King,
For You have given me all that I need:
Peace for the keeping,
A tranquil heart,
These are the abundant things of the kingdom,
Where You spoke I'd have true life.

Inspired Scripture: 1 John 4:18, Isaiah 26:3, Philippians 4:6-7, John 10:10

AN ADVENTUROUS PROMISE

We thank You, our Lord,
How Your goodness never ends,
It arches higher, wider, & brighter than any rainbow this world has ever seen!

Your kind words bring a fullness of life,
Especially on days that I find going my own way doesn't work.
In those times, You're so faithful to remind me,
That Your ways are so much higher than mine.

How there's a better way of living,
it is called the kingdom way:
Having faith in the one true living God,
Believing for things I cannot see here on earth.
How Your ways have so much thrill, adventure, & surprises,
Kind of like riding my bike!

Show me Your better way of living, my adventurous King!
Into Your hands, I commit my entire being,
Lead me to places I could never dream!

Inspired Scripture: Jeremiah 32:36-41, John 15:1-8,
Galatians 5:22-23, Isaiah 55:8-9

LiMiTLESS LoVE

Your love oh Lord,
It simply can't be measured!
How it extends higher than the heavens!

I desire to spend all my days here in Your presence,
Getting lost in Your gaze,
Face to face with You.

Better is one day here than all other places;
Both men & animals take refuge under Your glorious wings of protection.
You open Your hand, feeding all living things;
How You never fail to provide any good thing!

It's Your kindness that draws us closer,
Making it easier than ever to get lost in Your love,
A love that knows no limits.

Inspired Scripture: Psalm 36:5, Psalm 18:34, Psalm 25:10, Psalm 84:10

SAILING IN YOUR SEAS OF LOVE

Your love, oh Lord,
Brings a tranquil heart & mind.
For I am Yours,
& You'll always be mine.

Your love is like the great oceans,
It comes without borders.
You are so quick to forgive,
Showing a love that does not condemn.

May we always find ourselves resting in Your presence...
May we become more like You each day...
Sailing upon Your great seas of love!

Inspired Scripture: Proverbs 17:7, 1 John 5:15 , 1 Corinthians 13:4-7

DELIGHT IN YOU

Delight, delight...
Oh how I will delight in You, my sweet King!

I enjoy spending time with You,
It's here I find more of Your heart

You fill me with Your sweetness of life
Sprinkling Your joy & laughter
Making it easy to see,
That apart from You,
I have no good thing!

Inspired Scripture: Psalm 103, Psalm 37:4, Psalm 16:1-2

A MATE FOR LiFE

I sing to the King!
For He has brought me my mate for life;
A constant companion,
A faithful pal.
Your grace & patience towards me,
Surpasses any other friend.

God says to love at all times—
How you faithfully do,
Even when I am in an angry mood!

I can trust you with my secrets,
You protect my greatest dreams & desires.
By your faithful encouragement,
I'm able to venture into the great seas.

Thank you for always believing the best about me,
For always speaking words of life.
I love you,
My faithful companion,
How you are my mate for life!

Inspired Scripture: Ephesians 4:29, 1 Thessalonians 5:11, Hebrews 10:24-25

GOD GAVE ME YOU

Today I rejoice, today I sing!
Praising my good, good Father,
For giving me you!

How He said it wasn't good for me to be alone,
He knew I needed you,
More than I ever knew!

A faithful lover, a perfect friend,
One to explore His world with.
How I praise the God up above,
For giving me the priceless gift of you!

We may not always get it right,
& some days we miss the mark.
But because of His unfailing love,
There's great faith that we will make this work!

I can't wait for the days ahead...
Seeing each one unfold before our eyes,
Starting from the moment we place our feet out of bed.

Thank you for loving me both through the good & bad,
How you always reflect The King's love—
A love I have never received from a man!

How great are His promises for those who believe,
For they are always higher than I could dream!

How do I know this is true?
Because God gave me you!

A TiGER'S PROCLAMATiON

Today we play, today we sing,
We celebrate our loving Father,
The Great One who knows each of us by name!
Today, tomorrow, & light years beyond...
Is the promise that You are always good.

Your desire is for us to have joy;
You delight in hearing our laughter;
It puts a smile on Your face to see us pursue all the things of You,
The things of our great & glorious Father!

Friendship, kindness, & affection—
You're the one who gives it all.
How You are the greatest companion of them all!

Inspired Scripture: James 1:16-17, John 10:10, Proverbs 15:1, Romans 8:28

THE END!

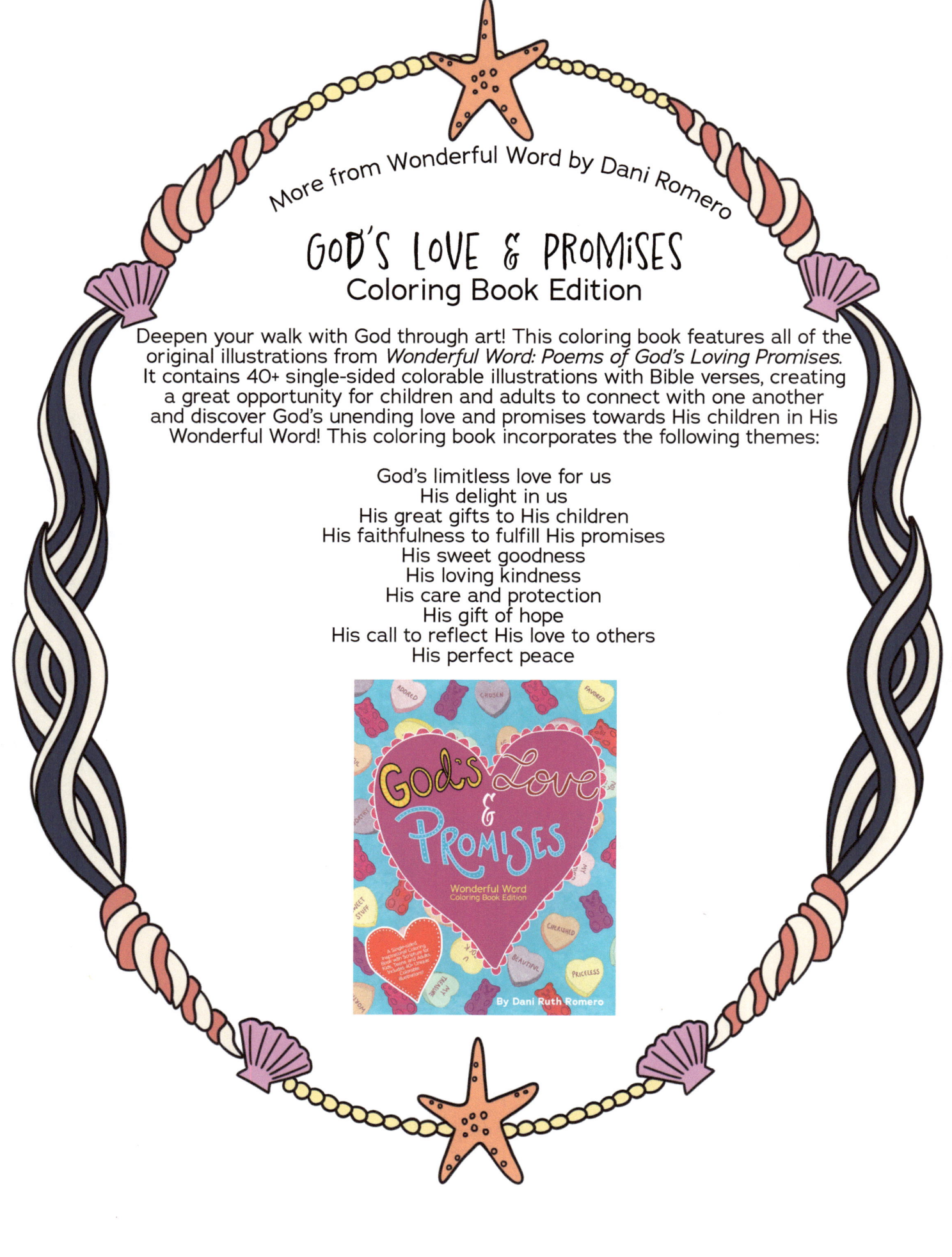

More from Wonderful Word by Dani Romero

GOD'S LOVE & PROMISES
Coloring Book Edition

Deepen your walk with God through art! This coloring book features all of the original illustrations from *Wonderful Word: Poems of God's Loving Promises*. It contains 40+ single-sided colorable illustrations with Bible verses, creating a great opportunity for children and adults to connect with one another and discover God's unending love and promises towards His children in His Wonderful Word! This coloring book incorporates the following themes:

God's limitless love for us
His delight in us
His great gifts to His children
His faithfulness to fulfill His promises
His sweet goodness
His loving kindness
His care and protection
His gift of hope
His call to reflect His love to others
His perfect peace

www.ingramcontent.com/pod-product-compliance
Lightning Source LLC
Chambersburg PA
CBHW041554120626
46551CB00002B/198